We live a long way from the sea and in the height of summer it can take many hours to reach the coast.

But the minute we catch a glimpse of the water, sparkling on the horizon, the cares of the journey disappear.

A brisk, salty breeze; clear, coastal light; and the sound of the seagulls whirling overhead - eyeing up our fish and chip supper – as we stroll along the pier and we are restored...

Nicola xx

Contents

Notes about Fabric..................5

Techniques...........................6

The Blocks

MockTurtle..............................8
Lifering.................................12
Dinghy..................................16
Fisherman's Cottage..............20
Seagull.................................24
Pilchards..............................28
Whale.................................. 32
Lighthouse............................36

Finishing the Quilt................41

Setting Sail...........................44

Sailing By Sampler Templates........45

Acknowledgement

Hearty thanks to first mate Kristal Jacobson for setting sail with me once more to test and edit this pattern.

Notes about Fabric

To make the Sailing By Sampler Quilt you will need the following:-

1 Fat Quarter each of red & grey blender prints
1 Fat Quarter of grey floral (for the Whale)
1 Fat Eighth of green blender print
1 Fat Eighth of multi small-scale floral
1 Fat Sixteenth each of yellow prints A & B and a red print (for the Dingy)
½ yd of white blender print
1½ yds **light** contrast (white)
2¾ yds **dark** contrast/block background (blue blender)
64" square of cotton batting
3½ yds backing fabric
½ yd of binding fabric
White and dark grey embroidery floss
Optional: a scrap of lightweight interfacing (for the Lifering).

Choosing fabrics...

The design for the blocks and the setting evolved together and I loved the idea of the Whale and the Lighthouse 'escaping' from their squares. The blocks are inspired by happy holidays to Cornwall and the setting by iconic Cornishware. Made since 1924 by TG Green Ltd, Cornishware is a distinctive shade of blue, which was the starting point for my colour scheme: those crisp blue and white stripes instantly bring back memories of sparkling waves and Mackerel skies.

Luckily, as I was designing my quilt blocks, Moda designer Linzee Kull McCray released a wonderful fabric collection called *True Blue*, which was based on 1930's Feedsack prints - following it up with a sister collection, *Red Rover* - so I knew I'd found the happy, vintage colour palette for my quilt. You, of course, may decide to reflect your own favourite coastal destination in your choice of background fabric and opt for smart Navy blue, tropical turquoise or a gentle seaglass.

I chose to compliment Linzee's prints with a pale grey Swiss dot, a dainty Liberty floral and a tiny grey Tilda star, to recall sun bleached timber, barnacle encrusted whales and salt speckled sailcloth.

Please note that individual requirements are listed with each block

Techniques

Snowballed corners

Snowballing the corner of a piece of fabric - by adding a 45° triangle of another fabric - gives the illusion of a rounded corner.

Start by marking a diagonal line on the back of a square of fabric. Pin it, right sides together, to a corner of the base fabric. Stitch on the line, flip the square 'open' and press, trimming away the back layers.

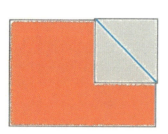
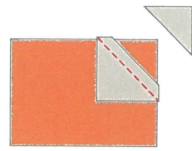
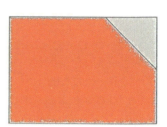

The Triangle-in-a-Square

The Triangle-in-a-Square technique creates an obtuse angle which helps us to achieve steep slate roofs, slippery fish and seagull beaks.

The first step is to prepare the side piece by trimming it down with a diagonal cut, offsetting the diagonal by ½" from one corner (discard the smaller portion). If you are creating a triangle (like the Pilchard's sharp snouts) you will to make a pair of mirror-image pieces, so place your side pieces right-sides-together before trimming..

The base piece is then marked with a placement line using either the large (LTS) or small (STS) Triangle-in-a-Square template. Position and pin a prepared side piece on the marked line. Then stitch ¼" away before flipping 'open' and pressing. Turn your block to the wrong side and trim the side piece and back layers, using the base piece as a guide.

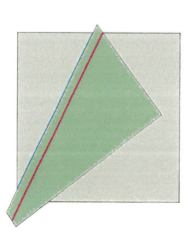

Creating other Angles

The Lighthouse, with its gently sloping sides, employs exactly the same technique as the Triangle-in-a-Square: first trimming down side pieces and then marking a placement line on the base fabric with a template. In this case the base fabric has been pieced to add windows, doors and cheery stripes to the Lighthouse stack.

Embroidery

All of the embroidery elements employ a simple back stitch, using 6-stranded cotton embroidery thread and an embroidery or chenille needle. The diagram shows the direction (→) of the stitches (•).

•9 → 10•7 → 8•5 → 6•3 → 4•1 → 2•

If you enjoy embroidery you could certainly add extra details: roses around the door of the Fisherman's Cottage or initials on the Dinghy sail. If it's not your favourite there are suggestions for replacing the embroidery on appropriate rows.

Quilting

I decided to hand quilt my sampler with a gentle wave motif and you will find the design along with all the other templates at the back of the book. You could also use the template to machine quilt, but if I have the time, there's nothing quite as relaxing as hand quilting, especially if it's on the beach accompanied by the sound of breaking waves.

Please read through the pattern before you begin, assuming a ¼" seam allowance and a fabric width (WOF) of 42". Pattern Corrections can be found on my website www.cakestandquilts.com

Mock Turtle

MATERIALS:

14" finished block

<u>1</u> Fat Quarter background fabric
5½" x 10" scrap of green for the turtle's body
5" x 10" scrap of contrast fabric **A**
5" square scrap of contrast fabric **B**

CUTTING:

1. From the background Fat Quarter cut as shown, below left:-

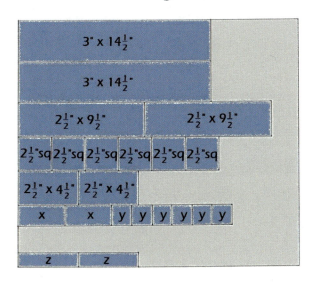

X = 1½" x 3½"
Y = 1½" square
Z = 1" x 4½"

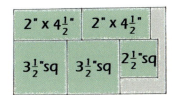

2. From the green fabric cut as shown, above right:-

3. From contrast fabric **A** cut <u>5</u> 2½" squares and a 1½" x 2½" piece.

4. From contrast fabric **B** cut <u>4</u> 2½" squares

PIECING THE BODY UNITS:

5. To make the head, draw or press a diagonal line on <u>2</u> 1½" background squares, pin one to a corner of the 2½" green square, stitch on the line, flip 'open' and press – to **snowball** the corner – trimming away the back pieces if preferred. Repeat on an adjacent corner, as shown, right.

6.   To make the left flipper, join a 1" x 4½" background piece to a 2" x 4½" green piece, then snowball the top left-hand corner with a 1½" background square and the lower right-hand corner with a 2½" square of contrast **A**, as shown, left.

7.   Repeat **step 6** to make the right flipper taking care to **REVERSE THE PLACEMENT**.

8.   To make the legs, snowball opposite corners of a 3½" green square with two 2½" background squares, then snowball one of the remaining corners with a 2½" square of contrast **A**, as shown. **MAKE 2**

9.   To make the base of the shell, snowball one side of the 1½" x 2½" contrast **A** piece with a 1½" background square, then repeat on the other side (to make a flying goose unit).

Then join to a contrast **B** square, pressing towards the square.

ASSEMBLING THE ROWS:

10.   Join a 2½" x 4½" background piece to each side of the head, pressing as directed (>)

11.   Join the flippers to each side of a 2½" contrast **B** square.

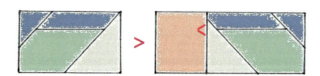

12. Create the centre of the shell by joining **2** 2½" background squares, **2** 2½" contrast **B** squares and the remaining 2½" contrast **A** square as shown below, pressing as directed.

13. Join the legs to each side of the base of the shell, pressing towards the shell, or open if preferred, before joining a 1½" x 3½" background piece to each side, pressing towards the background.

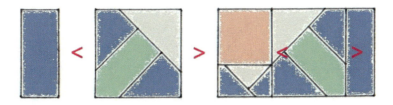

ASSEMBLING THE BLOCK:

14. Join the four rows together pressing the seams away from the flippers/legs, or open if preferred.

15. Join a 2½" x 9½" background piece to each side, pressing away from the Turtle, before joining a 3" x 14½" background piece to the top and bottom, again pressing away from the Turtle.

Your block should measure 14½" square.

Lifering

MATERIALS:

14" finished block

1 Fat Quarter background fabric
10" square of red fabric
10" square of white fabric
White & grey embroidery floss
Light-weight stabiliser

CUTTING:

1. From the background Fat Quarter cut as shown, below:-

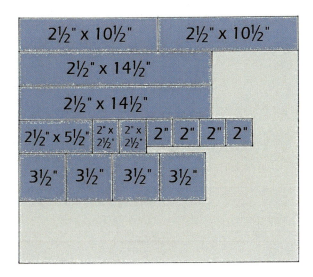

2. From the red fabric cut **2** 5" squares and **2** 2½" x 3" pieces

3. From the white fabric cut **2** 5" squares and **2** 2½" x 3" pieces

PIECING THE LIFERING:

6. Draw a diagonal line on the back of the white square, and pin - right sides together - to the red square. Stitch ¼" away from each side of your marked line; cut along that line and press open towards the red fabric to make two half-square triangle units (HSTs), as shown overleaf.

6.   Trim to 4½".

I do this by marking a 4½" square at the corner of my ruler with washi (low tack) tape, which makes it easier to line up my diagonals.

MAKE 2 PAIRS

7.   To make the outside corner of the lifebelt, mark a diagonal line on the back of a 3½" background, pin (right sides together) to the upper right-hand corner of a HST as shown. Stitch on the line, flip 'open' and press – **to 'snowball' the corner** – trimming away one or both of the back pieces, as preferred. Repeat on the opposite corner with a 2" square of background fabric. **MAKE 2**

8.   Repeat **step 7** taking care to reverse the placement, as shown right.

MAKE 2

9.   To make a centre unit, join a 2" x 2½" background piece to 2½" x 3" red piece, as shown left.

MAKE 2

10. To make the middle row join a 2½" x 3" white piece to each side of a 2½" x 5½" background piece.

MAKE 1

11. To assemble the lifering, join a corner unit to each side of a centre unit and then join those two rows to each side of the centre row, as shown right.

12. Then join a 2½" x 10½" background piece to each side and a 2½" x 14½" background piece to the top and bottom.

13. Apply the lightweight stabiliser to the areas being embroidered before monogram--ing the block using the embroidery template.

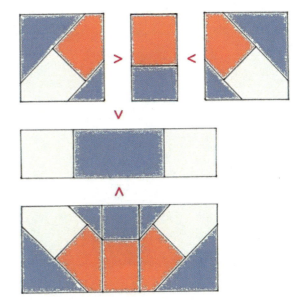

Your block should measure 14½" square.

Dinghy

MATERIALS:

14" finished block

<u>1</u> Fat Quarter background fabric
7½" square of white for the sail
1" x 8½" scrap of grey for the mast
2½" x 8½" scrap of coral for the boat

CUTTING:

1. From the background Fat Quarter cut as shown, below:-

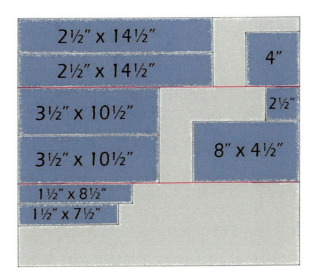

PIECING THE DINGHY:

2. Place the 4½" x 8" background piece on your cutting mat and, offsetting by ½" as shown below left, cut on the diagonal, discarding the smaller portion...

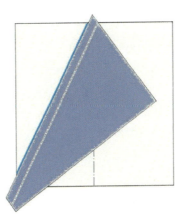

3.	Press the 7½" sail square in half and using the prepared **Dinghy template** placed on the centreline, mark a placement line then position the background piece on that placement line and stitch a ¼" away before flipping 'open' and pressing. Turn the sail to the wrong side and trim to size, using the background square as your guide.

4.	Mark a diagonal line on the 4" background square. Pin to the right-hand corner of the sail, stitch on the line, as shown below centre, flip 'open' and press – to 'snowball' the corner – trimming away the back pieces if preferred.

 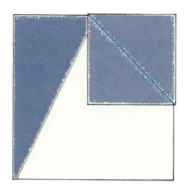

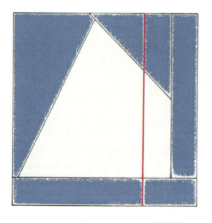

< 2½" >

5.	Join a 1½" x 7½" background piece to the right hand side (pressing away from the sail), as shown above right, then join a 1½" x 8½" background piece to the bottom (again pressing away from the sail), before cutting vertically through your sail unit 2½" away from the right-hand edge.

6.	Join the two halves of the sail unit to each side of 1" x 8½" mast piece, pressing towards the mast, then join the 2½" x 8½" dinghy piece to the bottom.

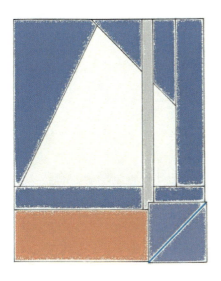

7. Create the prow of the dinghy by 'snowballing' the corner with a 2½" background square.

8. Assemble the block by joining a 3½" x 10½" piece to each side, then joining 2½" x 14½" piece to the top and bottom, pressing away from the dinghy.

Your block should measure 14½"

Fisherman's Cottage

MATERIALS:

14" finished block

1 Fat Quarter background fabric
10" square of grey roof fabric
10" square of white wall fabric
10" x 5" piece of a light print porch fabric
2½" x 5" piece of yellow window fabric
2½" x 3½" scrap of green for the door

CUTTING:

1. From the background Fat Quarter cut as shown, below left:-

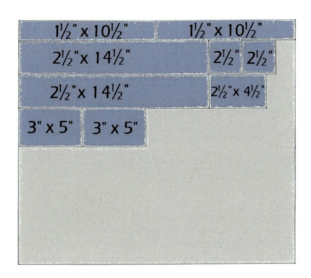
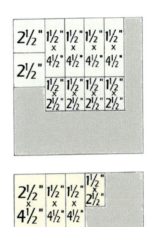

2. From the white wall fabric cut as shown, above top right:-

3. From the light print fabric cut as shown, above lower right:-

4. From the grey roof fabric cut **2** 4½" squares, **1** 2½" x 4½" pieces and **2** 2½" squares.

5. From yellow window fabric cut **2** 2½" squares.

PIECING THE COTTAGE:

6. To make the chimney unit join a 2½" white squire to 2½" background square, pressing as directed overleaf (>). **MAKE 2** then join to each side of a 2½" x 4½" background piece.

6. To make the porch roof, draw or press a diagonal line on **2** 2½" grey squares, pin one to a corner of the 2½" x 4½" print piece, stitch on the line, flip 'open' and press, trimming away the back pieces if preferred. Repeat on an adjacent corner, as shown, right.

7. To make the roof, join a 2½" x 4½" grey piece to the top of the porch roof, pressing away from the porch. Then join a 4½" square to each side, again pressing away from the porch.

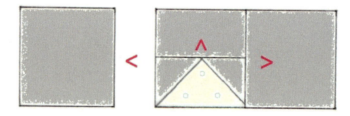

8. Place the pairs of 3" x 5" background pieces right sides together and – offsetting the diagonal by ½" (*) from one corner – trim, discarding the smaller portion, giving you a pair of mirror-image pieces.

 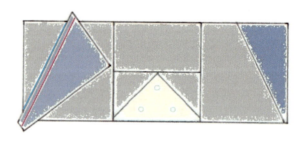

9. Assemble the roof by marking placement lines with the **LTS template** at each end of the roof unit then positioning and pinning the prepared background pieces on the line, as shown above. Stitch ¼" away before flipping 'open' and pressing. Turn your block to the wrong side and trim, using the roof unit as a guide.

10. To make the cottage front join a 1½" x 2½" wall piece to each side of the 2½" yellow squares, pressing towards the yellow. Then join the 1½" x 2½" print piece to the top of the door, pressing towards the door. Assemble the house with 1½" x 4½" print and wall pieces, as shown below, pressing towards the wall sections. **MAKE 4**

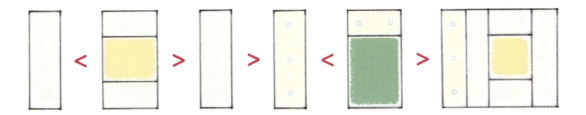

11. To assemble the cottage, join the chimney section, roof and cottage front, as shown right, pressing away from the roof.

Then join a 1½" x 10½" background piece to each side of the cottage and a 2½" x 14½" background piece to the top and bottom.

Your block should measure 14½" square.

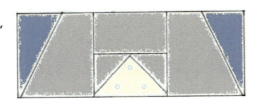

Seagull

MATERIALS:

14" finished block

1 Fat Quarter background fabric
5" x 8½" scrap of white for the seagull's body
4½" x 6½" scrap of grey for the wing
5" square scrap of yellow for the beak and legs
Grey embroidery floss

CUTTING:

1. From the background Fat Quarter cut as shown, below left:-

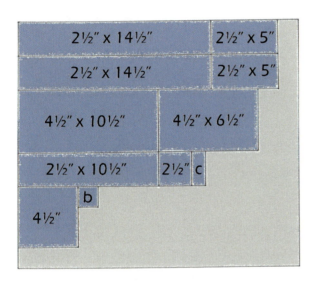

a = 2" x 3"
b = 1½" sq
c = 1" x 2½"

2. From the yellow scrap cut as shown, above right:-

3. From the white fabric cut **2** 2½" strips and subcut a 2½" x 8½" piece and **2** 2½" squares.

PIECING THE SEAGULL:

4. To make the Seagull's shoulder, mark a diagonal line on the back of a 2½" white square, pin one (right sides together) to the lower left-hand corner of the 4½" x 6½" background pieces, as shown overleaf. Stitch on the line, flip 'open' and press – **to 'snowball' the corner** – trimming away one or both of the back pieces if preferred.

 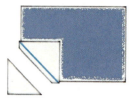 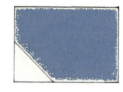

5. To make the Seagull's wing 'snowball' opposite corners of the 4½" x 6½" grey piece with a 4½" background square and a 2½" white square, taking care to position the squares correctly as shown in the diagram, right.

6. To make the Seagull's head 'snowball' opposite corners of the 2½" x 8½" white piece with 2½" and 1½" background. Again, check the placement carefully in the diagram.

7. To make the Seagull's beak use the **STS template** to mark a placement line on 4½" x 10½" background piece. Trim the 2" x 3" yellow piece diagonally - offsetting the diagonal by ½" from the lower left-hand corner - and place on the line, as shown below. Stitch ¼" away before flipping 'open' and pressing. Turn your block to the wrong side and trim, using the background piece as a guide.

½"

8. To make the Seagull's legs 'snowball' the lower right-hand corner of a 2½" x 5" background piece with a 1½" yellow square (**a**) to make a foot, then join a 1" x 2½" yellow piece (**b**) and a 1" x 2½" background piece (**c**), pressing away from the foot. Again 'snowball' the lower right-hand corner with a 1½" yellow square (**d**) and join the remaining 1" x 2½" yellow piece (**e**). Finally, join a 2½" x 5" background piece and trim the block to 2½" x 8½" (**f**).

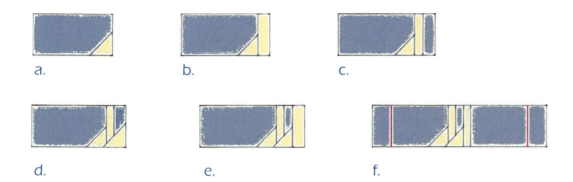

a.   b.   c.

d.   e.   f.

9.  Assemble the Seagull by joining the wing to the bottom of the shoulder, pressing towards the shoulder. Join the head to the body, pressing towards the head, before joining the legs, pressing towards the body or open if preferred. Then join the beak to the head, pressing towards the head. Finally, join a 2½" x 10½" background piece to the right side of the block and a 2½" x 14½" piece to the top & bottom, pressing away from the seagull.

10. Using the photo as a guide, backstitch the eyelid using the embroidery floss.

Your block should measure 14½" square.

Pilchards

MATERIALS:

14" finished block

1 Fat Quarter background fabric
10" square of white fabric
1½" x 10" scraps of **3** contrast fabrics **A, B & C**
Grey embroidery floss

CUTTING:

1.   From the background Fat Quarter cut as shown, below left:-

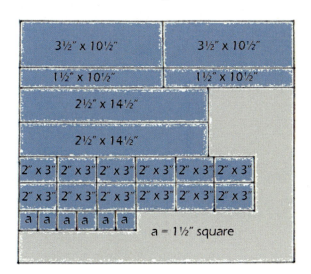

2.   From the white fabric cut as shown, above right:-

3.   From contrast **A, B & C** fabric strips cut a 1½" x 7" piece and a 1½" x 2½" piece.

PIECING THE PILCHARD UNITS:

4.   Join a 1½" x 7" white piece to a 1½" x 7" contrast **A** piece, pressing the seam open. Then join a 2½" x 3" white piece to one end, pressing as directed (>).

 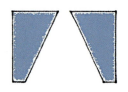

5. Prepare a pair of 2" x 3" background pieces by placing them right sides together and – offsetting the diagonal by ½" (*) from one corner – trim, discarding the smaller portion, giving you a pair of mirror-image pieces.

*

MAKE 6 PAIRS

6. Create the Pilchard's body by marking placement lines with the **STS template** at each end then positioning and pinning the prepared background pieces on the line...

...stitch ¼" away before flipping 'open' and pressing. Turn your unit to the wrong side and trim, using the background rectangle as a guide.

7. To make the Pilchard's tail, draw or press a diagonal line on **2** 1½" background squares, pin one to a corner of the 1½" x 2½" print piece, stitch on the line, flip 'open' and press, trimming away the back pieces. Repeat on an adjacent corner, as shown, left.

8. Join the tail to the end of the Pilchard's body, pressing the seam open.

MAKE 1

9. Repeat **steps 4 - 8** with contrast fabrics **B**.

MAKE 1

10. Repeat **steps 4 - 8** with contrast fabrics **C, REVERSING THE PLACEMENT.**

MAKE 1

ASSEMBLING THE BLOCK:

10. Arrange the Pilchards in alternating directions with the 1½" x 10½" background pieces in between and join together, pressing towards the background.

11. Join a 3½" x 10½" background piece to each side and a 2½" x 14½" background piece to the top and bottom, pressing away from the Pilchards.

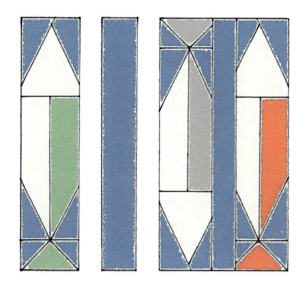

12. Using the photo as a guide, backstitch the eyelid using the embroidery floss.

Your block should measure 14½" square.

Whale

MATERIALS:

14" x 28" finished block

¼ yd background fabric
¼ yd white fabric
1 Fat Quarter scrap of grey fabric
Dark grey embroidery floss

CUTTING:

1. From the background fabric cut as shown below:-

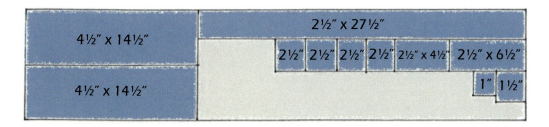

2. From the white fabric cut **2** 2½" x WOF strips and subcut **1** 2½" x 27½", **1** 2½" x 14½", **1** 2½" x 10½" and **1** 2½" square.

3. From the grey Fat Quarter cut as shown, left:-

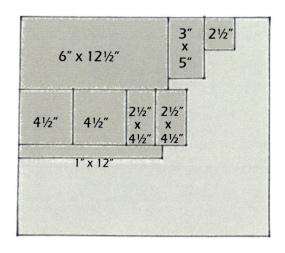

PIECING THE WHALE'S HEAD:

4. To make the head, join the 1" background square to the end of the 1" x 12" grey strip to create the mouth, then join to the bottom of the 6" x 12½" grey piece, pressing away from the mouth.

5. Draw or press a diagonal line on a 1½" background squares, pin to the top left-hand corner of the whale's head, stitch on the line, flip 'open' and press – to **snowball** the corner – trimming away the back pieces if preferred.

6. To make the flipper, snowball the top right-hand corner of a 4½" x 14½" background piece with a 2½" grey square.

7. Join a 2½" x 6½" background piece to the left of the Whale's head, pressing towards the background, the remaining 4½" x 14½" background piece to the top and the flipper unit to the bottom, pressing towards the Whale.

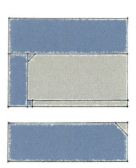

PIECING THE WHALE'S TAIL:

8. Make a strip-set by joining the 2½" x 27½" white and background strips, pressing towards the background. Subcut **1** 14½" section and **2** 6½" sections.

9. To make the upper fluke, snowball one end of a 2½" x 4½" grey piece with a 2½" background square, taking care with the placement, as shown right. Then snowball the other end with a 2½" white square.

10. Prepare the 3" x 5" grey piece by trimming diagonally, offsetting the diagonal by ½" (*) from one corner as shown. Discard the smaller portion.

*

34

11. Mark a placement line with the **LTS template** at the end of a 6½" section of strip set then positioning & pinning the prepared grey piece on the line, right sides together. Stitch ¼" away from that line before flipping 'open' and pressing. Turn to the wrong side and trim, using the strip-set unit as a guide.

12. Join the trimmed unit to left side of the fluke and the remaining 6½" section of strip-set to the right, pressing away from the fluke.

13. To make the lower fluke, snowball each end of the remaining 2½" x 4½" grey piece with 2½" background square, taking care with the placement, as shown right

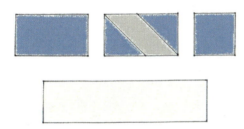

14. Join a 2½" x 4½" background piece to the left side and a 2½" square to the right side – as shown - and pressing away from the fluke. Then join the 2½" x 10½" white piece to the bottom, pressing towards the white, or open if preferred.

15. Snowball the top left-hand corner with a 4½" square and then join the remaining 4½" grey square, pressing away from the fluke.

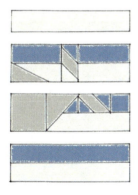

16. Assemble the tail by joining the two fluke units together, pressing towards the lower fluke or open of preferred. Then join the 14½" section of strip-set - made in **step 8** - to the bottom and the 2½" x 14½" white piece to the top, pressing towards the tail.

ASSEMBLING THE BLOCK:

14. Join the Whale' head to its tail, pressing the seam open, and using the photo as a guide embroider the Whale's eye in backstitch.

Your block should measure 14½" x 28½"

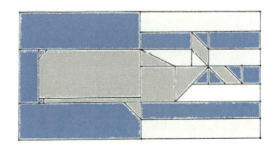

Lighthouse

MATERIALS:

14" x 28" finished block

½ yd background fabric
¼ yd white (plus **1** Fat Eighth if stack is different)
10" square of red fabric
2 2½" x 7" scraps of yellow lantern fabric
5" x 6" scrap of grey roof fabric
2½" x 3½" scrap of green door fabric

CUTTING:

1. From the background fabric cut **1** 4½" x WOF strip and subcut **2** 4½" x 12½" pieces.
Then cut **2** 2½" x WOF strips and subcut **1** 2½" x 27½" piece, **1** 2½" x 14½" piece, **2** 2½" x 13½" pieces, **2** 2½" x 4½" pieces and, from the trimmings, **2** 1½" squares.

2. From the white fabric cut as shown below:-

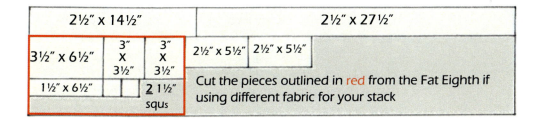

3. From the red fabric, cut as shown right.

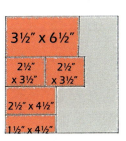

4. From each of the yellow fabrics (A & B) cut **1** 2½" square, **2** 1½" x 2½" pieces and, from the trimmings of one fabric only, **1** 1½" square.

5. From the grey fabric cut **2** 3" x 5" pieces.

PIECING THE LANTERN:

6. Make a strip-set by joining the 2½" x 27½" white and background strips, pressing towards the background. Subcut **2** 7½" sections and **2** 5½" sections.

7. Prepare the 3" x 5" grey pieces by placing them right sides together and trimming diagonally, offsetting the diagonal by ½" (*) from one corner as shown. Discard the smaller portion.

 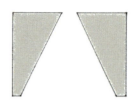

*

8. To make the right-hand portion of the roof, mark a placement line with the **LTS template** at the end of a 7½" section of strip set, as shown overleaf, then positioning and pinning the prepared grey piece on the line, right sides together. Stitch ¼" away from that line before flipping 'open' and pressing. Turn to the wrong side and trim, using the strip-set unit as a guide.

9. Repeat **step 8** to make the left-hand portion of the roof taking care to **REVERSE THE PLACEMENT**. Then join the two halves together, pressing the seam open.

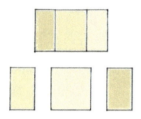

10. To make the lantern, join a 1½" x 2½" yellow **A*** piece to each side of a 2½" yellow **B*** square, pressing towards the centre square. Repeat with the remaining yellow pieces, this time pressing away from the centre square. Next, join the two rows together, pressing the seam open. Then add a 5½" section of strip-set to each side.

*Try turning some of your yellow pieces to the wrong side to vary the shades of yellow and give your lantern extra sparkle.

11. Make the parapet by joining a 1½" background square to each side of the 1½" x 4½" red piece, pressing towards the background.

12. Next, join to a 1½" x 6½" white piece, pressing away from the white or open if preferred. Then join a 2½" x 4½" background piece to each side, pressing towards the background.

13. Join a 2½" x 5½" white piece to each side of the 2½" x 4½" red piece, pressing towards the red, then join to the bottom of the parapet.

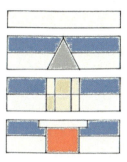

14. Assemble the lantern by joining the roof row to the lantern row, then adding the parapet to the bottom and a 2½" x 14½" white strip to the top. Press the seams towards the background stripes or open if preferred.

PIECING THE TOWER:

15. To make the door, join a 2½" x 3½" red piece to each side of the 2½" x 3½" door piece, pressing towards the door.

16. To make the window, join a 1½" white square to each side of the 1½" yellow square, pressing towards the yellow. Then join a 3" x 3½" white piece to each side, pressing away from the window.

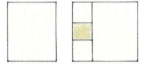

17. Assemble the tower by joining the remaining 3½" x 6½" red and white pieces, then adding the door unit to the bottom and the window section to the top, alternating red and white sections and pressing towards the red.

18. Prepare the 2½" x 13½" background pieces by placing them right sides together and trimming diagonally, offsetting the diagonal by 1" (*) from one corner, as shown below left. Discard the smaller portion.

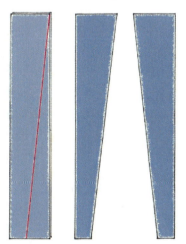

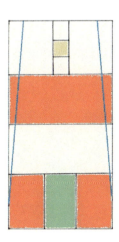

*

19. Mark placement lines on the tower with the upper and lower halves of the **Lighthouse template**, as shown above right, then position and pin the prepared background pieces on the line, right sides together. Stitch ¼" away from that line before flipping 'open' and pressing. Turn to the wrong side and trim, using the tower unit as a guide.

20. Join a 4½" x 12½" background piece to each side and a 2½" x 14½" piece to the bottom, pressing away from the tower.

ASSEMBLING THE BLOCK:

14. Join the lantern to the tower, pressing the seam open.

Your block should measure 14½" x 28½"

Finishing the Quilt

The graphic setting blocks are very simple to construct and, whilst I hesitate to tell you how to sew strips of fabric together, I do have some tips on cutting your fabric and, of course, how much you'll need.

CUTTING:

1. Although we will be cutting 2½" strips from our blue and white fabric we won't be cutting them across the width of the fabric, as we might usually do, as this will result in a lot of waste. Instead we are going to make the best use of our fabric by cutting 14½" x WOF strips and subcutting the 2½" strips we need.

2. From the dark contrast/background cut <u>18</u> 2½" x 14½" strips as shown:-

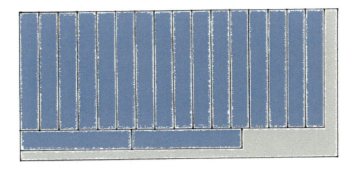

3. From the light contrast fabric cut <u>24</u> 2½" x 14½" strips as shown overleaf:-

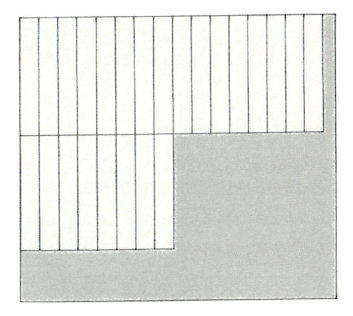

Note: there will be some fabric left, but it's a very usable piece.

PIECING THE STRIPY BLOCKS:

4. For each block you will need <u>4</u> 2½" x 14½" light contrast strips and <u>3</u> 2½" x 14½" dark contrast strips. Join the strips, alternating the dark and light fabrics and pressing towards the dark fabric. Your block should measure 14½" square.

MAKE <u>6</u>

ASSEMBLING THE QUILT:

5. Position the Whale and Lighthouse blocks in opposite corners then arrange the remaining <u>12</u> blocks - alternating the Sampler and stripy blocks - to form the quilt centre. Join the top right <u>6</u> blocks in two rows of three, pressing as directed (>). Then join to the Lighthouse, pressing the seam towards the Lighthouse or open if preferred.

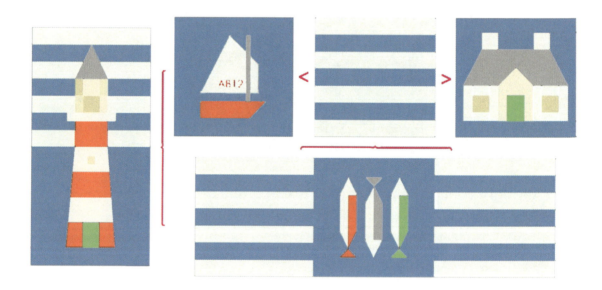

6. Join the three rows together – as shown overleaf - pressing your seams to the side or open, as you prefer.

7. Cut the backing fabric into two 62" x WOF pieces. Trim off the selvages and join together using a ½" seam, pressed open, then trim to 62" square.

8. Sandwich the batting between the backing and the quilt top, baste, then machine or hand quilt.

9. Join your binding strips and press in half, wrong sides together, along its length. Trim away excess batting and background - taking the opportunity to ensure your corners are square - and bind the raw edge using your preferred method.

The Whale and Lighthouse blocks – which have escaped from the 14" square format - can both be used individually as a mini quilt or table runner, as follows:-

From ½ yd of backing fabric, cut <u>1</u> 18" x 32" piece. Sandwich an 18" x 32" piece of cotton batting between the backing and the block, baste, then machine or hand quilt.

From ¼ yd binding fabric, cut <u>3</u> 2¼" strips, join them to form one long piece and press in half - wrong sides together - along its length. Trim away excess batting and background - taking the opportunity to ensure your corners are square - and bind the raw edge using your preferred method.

Setting Sail

Any of the Sailing By sampler blocks can be used, either singly or combined, in smaller projects. My *Petit* FOUR series of projects (available at www.cakestandquilts.com) are designed to make use of one block, such as the Happy Wanderer bag, shown below left with the Mock Turtle block or the Cornish Cushion, shown below right with the Seagull block.

Pair the Happy Wanderer bag with Lifering block and line it with waterproof nylon fabric to make your child a swimming bag, embroidered with their initials; combine the Dinghy, the Lighthouse and a filler block to make a fun floor cushion to curl up and read *Treasure Island* on; or make a fabulous bolster cushion with the Whale block, perfect for reclining on at the beach, or adding a little Nantucket chic to your sofa.

Five blocks – combined with four filler blocks or large squares of a nautical print - would make a lovely baby quilt, finishing at 42" square or a little larger with a border. Again, baby's initials and date of birth could be embroidered on the Lifering or the Dinghy's sail.

Let your imagination set sail...

Lifering Embroidery Template

Trace onto the fabric or use with a light box.

ABCDEFG
HIJKLMNO
PQRSTUV
WXYZ123
4567890

Dinghy Template

Copy the template onto template plastic/card or use with a lightbox

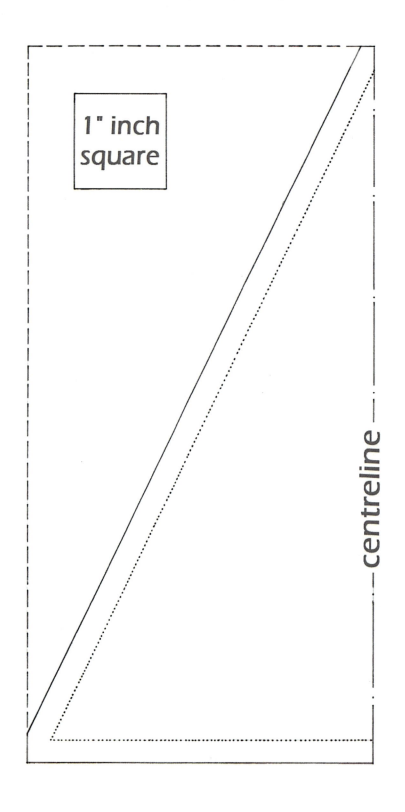

LTS Template

Copy the template onto template plastic/card or use with a light box.

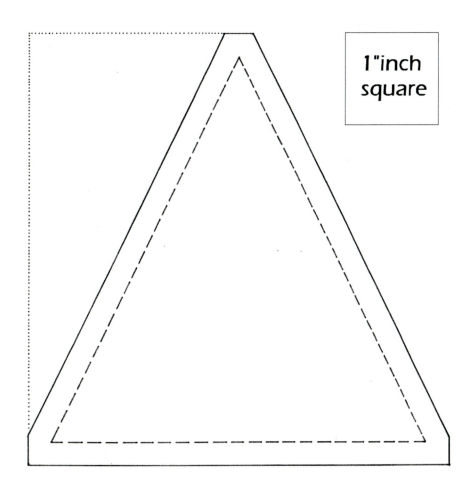

STS Template

Copy the template onto template plastic/card or use with a light box.

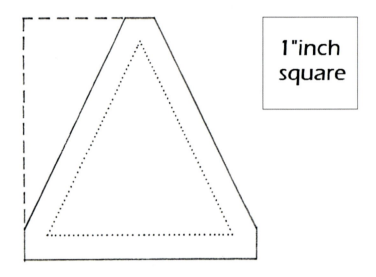

Upper Half of Lighthouse Template

Copy the template onto template plastic/card or use with a light box.

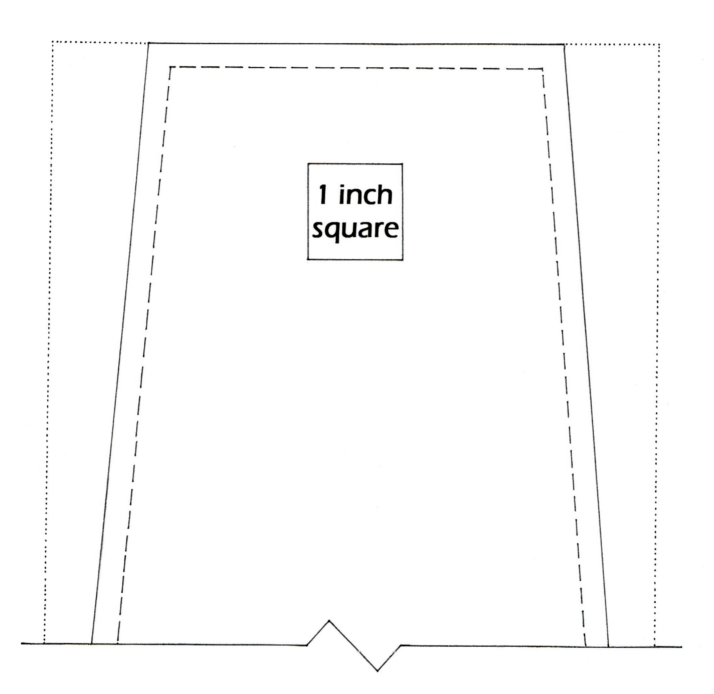

Lower Half of Lighthouse Template

Copy the template onto template plastic/card or use with a light box.

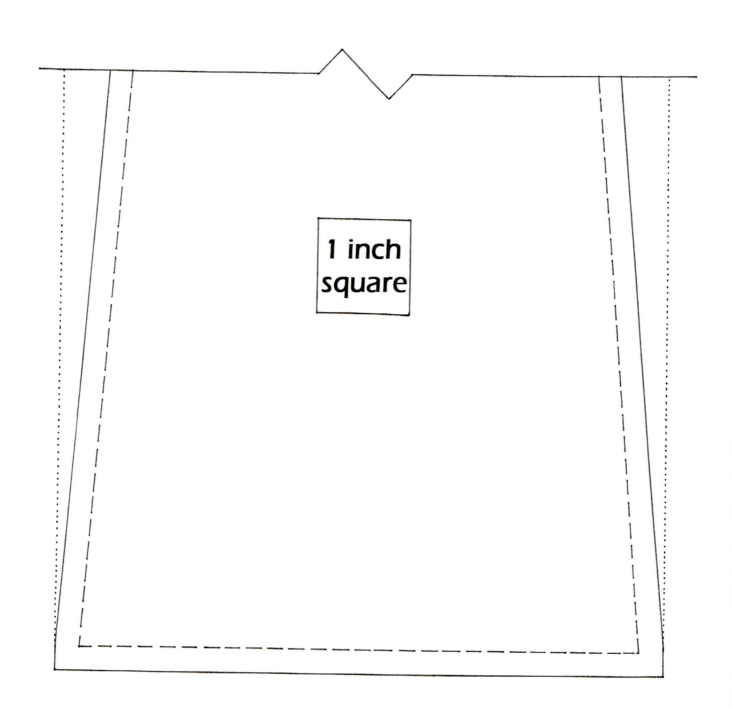

Quilting Template

Made in the USA
Middletown, DE
04 May 2022